Mandala Gardens

Inspired by

Tarthang Tulku

Peta

First published 1991

Copyright © 1991 by Dharma Publishing
Photographs by Jim McNulty
Maps drawn by Bill Farthing

Printed in USA by Dharma Enterprises, Oakland, California

ISBN: 0-945798-65-2

Contents

Preface

*O*ne spring afternoon this year, when the poppies were glowing orange against royal blue skies, the idea of a book on the Odiyan gardens came up. I was discussing various projects with Arnaud Maitland, the manager of Dharma Enterprises. I gave Arnaud and Jim McNulty permission to photograph the gardens, and the resulting pictures were compellingly beautiful. In the past, we have rarely released photographs of Odiyan, for it is a private retreat center. Now it seemed that publication of a book about the Odiyan gardens would serve several good purposes.

For the last few years, Dharma Enterprises has made great efforts to support our projects at Odiyan. Giving them permission to distribute such a work through their Amber Lotus Division would be a way to express my gratitude. Part of the proceeds from the book could also be dedicated to Odiyan projects. Odiyan's supporters and friends would appreciate a book on the gardens that their efforts had helped create.

Beautiful pictures might express something difficult to put into words, something important to remember today—the heartfelt connection between nature and human being.

In several discussions early this summer, I shared some of my thoughts about the mandala gardens and the power of natural beauty. Dharma Publishing helped prepare a manuscript, and Leslie Bradburn took editorial responsibility.

From the very first beginnings of Odiyan, I envisioned parkland and gardens surrounding the main buildings. Originally overgrazed and logged, the Odiyan land has come back to life over the last sixteen years, returning to us bountiful rewards for our efforts. Gradually, we have created extensive formal gardens with roses, rhododendrons, gardenias, wisterias, and many other varieties of plants.

Each year we have added thousands of seeds and thousands of plantings to the natural landscape and reforested many acres. We have been very fortunate to have good weather, water, and soil, and year by year we have seen improvement. The gardens around the Stupa and the landscaping around Tibetan Hill and Yeshe Tsogyal Lake have become especially colorful and fragrant, and are visited by many wild birds. The dream is coming true in the form of the mandala gardens.

I would like to thank all of those who have made the beauty of the mandala gardens possible through their care and support. Students from Nyingma Institute and Dharma Press sponsored the planting of many exotic trees. Barry Schieber, Alicia Fazio, Bill Farthing, and Katie Pence have taken an abiding interest in the Odiyan landscaping, spending long hours, rain or shine, caring for the gardens. Barr and June Rosenberg helped us expand the Stupa gardens by sponsoring the planting of many hundreds of rose bushes.

After a fire in the orchards, several nurseries donated trees for replanting. People from the Nyingma centers in Germany, Holland, and Brazil have come several summers to work on the land.

Gradually, the Odiyan gardens are developing into true botanical gardens that include rare plants from around the world as well as those from California. Since they bloom in different seasons depending on their native habitats, unusual flowers and foliage can be found any time of year in different locations.

On long walks winding around Tibetan Hill, we have found herbs and medicinal plants. These discoveries raise the possibility of creating an extensive herb garden that could be both culinary and medical. Our long-range plans for a health care clinic might include such experimental gardens where we could grow medicinal herbs from the Himalayas and various other regions of the Tibetan Plateau.

Even though we have many large projects underway at once, we are committed to protecting the Odiyan gardens for the future. Much work remains to be done, for the gardens, especially around the Vajra Temple, are not all complete, and the task of simply maintaining what has already been developed requires a substantial amount of time and energy.

Anyone who wishes to contribute to the work is welcome. The projects at Odiyan have been developed through the support of individuals who have graciously made contributions in different ways. Working in the Odiyan mandala gardens is an opportunity to participate in bringing a vision into reality—a uniquely balanced vision that unites spiritual and practical realities and harmonizes the beauty of nature with the beauty of sacred art and architecture. There is so much to learn about how the universal mandala comes alive. The opportunities for knowledge are truly boundless.

Over the years, our work at Odiyan has yielded a great deal of practical experience, and in time it may be possible to produce a book that details our way of working on the land. My present concern, however, has not been to create a practical manual. In this volume, what I wish to share is my appreciation for the mandala gardens and my way of observing nature and human nature. What I have learned from the flowers, you too might discover.

Tarthang Tulku
Berkeley
Fall 1991

Introduction

*O*diyan retreat center, located in northern California, was founded in 1975. From the beginning, the land has been an integral part of the vision and development of Odiyan. There, nature overflows with variety, offering us ocean, mountains, forest, fields, dramatic seasons, and a kaleidoscopic beauty that changes day by day.

The power and beauty of the environment create a support for spiritual endeavors. Inner spiritual realities are reflected in the colors, shapes, and forms of the outer natural world. This relationship can be embodied and intensified in the pattern known in the Buddhist tradition as a mandala, an aesthetic and symbolic arrangement of elements around a central point.

Individuals in Western culture have not yet had the opportunity to study in depth the principles and symbolism of the Buddhist mandala. Yet each of us has a natural receptivity to beauty and can appreciate aesthetic balance, rich colors, and striking elegant shapes without any special training.

The world of nature speaks to the human heart directly: We find ourselves already surrounded by beauty, naturally integrated into the field of the mandala.

Without any commentary or explanation, we can walk through a garden and feel the fullness of the experience. Colors and shapes delight the eyes, fragrance pours forth and enters our being as though we were drinking nectar. Sensations impress themselves upon the heart, communicating to human consciousness.

Sustained, nourished, and supported by beauty, the heart begins to open, like the petals of a flower unfolding. The flower of the heart is the center of a mandala. When the heart opens, we begin to realize the unity of existence and our communion with nature.

Cherishing beauty is the secret key to opening the heart, and once the heart opens, compassion and caring flow forth naturally. Thus, the world of nature has a crucial role to play in the development of the human values of compassion, love, and kindness.

Love and appreciation translate into understanding and action. If we appreciate nature, we take responsibility by tracing out the consequences of various lines of action. We consider the evidence and educate ourselves toward a more global perspective so that we are capable of protecting what we value.

Our relationship with nature offers us two precious opportunities: to receive beauty and to foster it. Both are equally important, for by protecting and preserving the field of beauty that offers nourishment for the heart, we serve the highest human values. If the realm of nature were to disappear, leaving us only the manufactured world of human making, our civilization could scarcely be called human. When we fall into the trap of thinking "civilized" and "natural" are opposites, then to become more civilized, we must control or conquer nature.

A view based on opposition, however, is limited, for the inner and outer environments are interdependent partners. The Buddhist tradition emphasizes harmony between humanity and nature and the importance of cultivating nonviolent attitudes and actions.

The teachings of the Buddha demonstrate that most of our troubles arise from lack of harmony at a deep level: judgmental and divisive intentions that emerge from the need for control, the greed for power, and a fundamental discrimination between subject and object.

The heart can sense lack of harmony and lack of completeness, and the head can foresee the negative consequences that will follow. We do not need philosophical discourses or religious instruction to know this much: that we have ignored something important and that this ignoring may lead to danger. But how can we let ourselves acknowledge and act upon this knowledge of our own ignoring? If we let beauty instruct us, we can recover wholeness and balance.

On one occasion the Buddha taught the path to Enlightenment by simply holding up a flower. Around the world, the flower is a well-known symbol for the soul. The lotus in the East and the rose in the West symbolize the blossoming of beautiful qualities, the wonder of love and compassion, and the mystery of spiritual communion.

Any of us can work with natural beauty, no matter where we live or how far from nature our lifestyle may be. We can become acquainted with a flower or plant and watch it flourish as we care for it. Shining with colors and sculpting elegant shapes, the light of beauty brings the knowledge of balance and harmony into our lives. If our spirit darkens, and we grow uncertain whether love and beauty remain in the world today, we can simply spend time in a garden or woods, and then inquire of our heart.

Here at Odiyan the mandala gardens are symbolic of our work, overflowing with abundant creativity, inspired by love. We have thus far planted five thousand roses, but we wish we could offer 500,000, a symbol of the great compassion and open-heartedness we seek to manifest. This unconditional love is like the love of Mother Nature, love that allows all of us to manifest. She grants us the freedom to act and express ourselves, to enjoy and appreciate the expressions of others. Unpossessive and unbounded, this open-ended accommodation continuously supports all forms of life.

May the readers of this book find for themselves forms of expression that enrich their lives.

Tarthang Tulku
Odiyan
Spring 1991

Dedicated to
the Mother of the Universe,
who has allowed me
the freedom
to express myself.
May the merit
of this work
bring happiness
and understanding
to others,
unfolding beauty and love
like the petals of a flower.

The Kingdom of Oddiyana

Many centuries ago in Asia, hidden in the deep valleys of the Hindukush mountains, was a kingdom known as Oddiyana. The royal capital was a holy city where a lineage of wise and inspired kings had ruled for several thousand years. Its stately palaces sparkled in the sun.

Standing by the windows at the uppermost tier of the highest palace, King Indrabhuti of Oddiyana caught sight of a most marvelous display: five hundred saffron-robed monks flying eastward, like a huge flock of rare birds. Inquiring of his ministers who these magical beings might be, the king

learned that they were the disciples of one known as the Buddha, he who had found the way to complete Enlightenment, he who had vanquished all obstacles to knowledge and freedom.

Journeying to the heavenly realms attended by his retinue, Shakyamuni Buddha was soaring through the skies above the kingdom of Oddiyana this very day.

Desiring to meet ones possessed of such power, the king ordered a great table be laid and commanded the ministers to find a way to invite the Buddha and his monks to the palace for a feast. They immediately arranged the performance of ceremonies atop the palace. Robed in finest silk, making the most heart-felt offerings, they deeply contemplated the wondrousness of these monks and wished fervently for their presence.

One by one the monks began to float down from the sky onto the top of the palace until at last the Buddha himself arrived, radiating light that bathed the whole palace in a golden glow. King Indrabhuti reverently approached and surrounded the Buddha with offerings, prayers, and perfumes, washed his feet, and offered the great feast to the monks.

Then Indrabhuti opened his heart to the Buddha:
"How can I become like you, Enlightened One?
How can one such as I obtain the power and blessings
of Enlightenment?"

Some say the king was well-prepared to hear the teachings
through previous lives of devotion to the Dharma. Others say
Indrabhuti was an extraordinarily intelligent individual
who could comprehend the highest teachings. An ordinary
person would renounce the worldly way of life, kingdom or
family, all status and wealth to follow the Dharma. But
Indrabhuti chose to remain in his palace, with his queen
and ministers, and there requested the highest teachings
that could bring full realization.

The Omniscient One, the Leader of Men, understood at once the mind of Indrabhuti. Transforming himself, the Buddha became invisible to all but the most advanced disciples and the king, whose consciousness was open to the teachings.

The king sensed directly the compassion of the Buddha, the depths of his wisdom, and the beauty of the glorious light body before him.

Touched by the pure power of the Buddha, the king's physical embodiment also changed into light, and with that light body he listened to the teachings of Enlightenment.

The voice of the Buddha transformed Indrabhuti's consciousness, and he passed through extraordinary meditative states one by one, until he was completely freed from all attachments.

*"The colors and shapes of appearance
mirror the inner light
of the Buddha"*

As his heart opened wide and his senses merged with light, the king beheld everything as radiantly beautiful, and his being was filled with bliss. The kingdom revealed itself as a perfect heavenly realm free from all human sufferings, and the beauty of the natural world became vividly apparent: The colors and shapes of appearance mirrored the inner light of the Buddha.

Indrabhuti transmitted this ecstatic vision of beauty and love to his queen and ministers. As these individuals spread the vision to others, the consciousness of the inhabitants of the kingdom began to change.

Infused with the light of beauty, body, speech, and mind became harmonized, and the pain of suffering was healed.

The inner nature of the human body, the outer nature of the environment, and the secret nature of consciousness united.

This knowledge purified the consciousness of everyone in the kingdom of Oddiyana and the entire population flew to heavenly realms.

Over time, people came once again to live in the valley. With the knowledge lineage firmly established there, the inhabitants again became transformed and joined the light of consciousness. It is said that several times in history, the population of Oddiyana completely disappeared.

This remarkable kingdom known as Oddiyana was located in a valley in the northwestern corner of the Indian subcontinent. An ancient sacred land, it is connected with the oldest civilizations on earth and the highest teachings of the Buddha, the Vajrayana, the lineage of Diamond Light.

From Oddiyana, the Vajrayana teachings were transmitted to India, the teachings of inner light flowing through continuous lineages of visionary masters. Oddiyana is also the birthplace of Padmasambhava, the Tantric Master who established Buddhism in Tibet in the eighth century. There, for more than twelve hundred years, the Buddhist teachings were preserved, encircled by the highest mountains on earth.

Our Relationship to the Earth

*A*s intelligent life on this planet, we have an obligation to care for the earth as a whole. We share the same space and time with other living species and interact with the atmosphere, the seas, and the environment. Yet we do not consider these other life forms our close friends. Swept up in the speed and pressures of the technological age, we neglect the natural world and have forgotten how to respect it. This lack of respect has become crucial today, a clear reflection of our human confusion and misunderstanding.

According to Tibetan Buddhist cosmology, humans inhabit only one of five or six realms of living beings. One of these other realms includes the kingdom of the nagas, creatures of the depths, the oceans and subterranean regions. The nagas are responsible for the environment, for weather and global water and wind cycles; they represent the great wealth of the earth, guarding natural resources and promoting the growth of all plant and animal life. Among the eight great naga kings, one rules the Pacific Ocean, and one the Atlantic. The Pacific symbolizes creative energy and the Atlantic the energy of power. Together these two protect the dynamic of the planet's environment.

The system of the nagas has direct impact on the world that human beings inhabit. When the nagas are satisfied, nature becomes abundant, harmonious, and beautiful. Flowers, fruits, greenery, fields of grain, and natural resources such as minerals, oil, gold, and silver all belong to the overflowing treasury of the nagas. When the nagas are ill or disturbed, nature goes out of balance, rain does not fall, earthquakes, hurricanes, and floods abound.

The energy generated by human activities can affect the naga kingdom positively and negatively. War is upsetting to the nagas; human beings struggling with one another over natural resources is deeply disturbing. The killing of animals or polluting the oceans and atmosphere causes imbalances for the nagas. Such destructive, greedy actions set in motion disturbances that result eventually in famine and disease.

Buddhist cosmology describes how the various kinds of beings are linked together: The jealous asuras and the heavenly gods struggle with one another; similarly, the nagas and the humans are potential antagonists. This antagonism could become instead a partnership if we recognized the forces of nature that the nagas embody.

Disconnected from the larger cosmos, unaware of entire realms of nature, we have become destructive without understanding the damage we are doing.

Destruction of nature reflects back to our human consciousness, which grows darker and more cloudy, like the polluted atmosphere surrounding our planet.

Today people are growing increasingly uneasy in the wake of the destruction of the environment. The modern way of life seems unaccommodating and ill-suited to the planet and human beings in many ways.

Our uneasiness, however, does not necessarily help us find harmony with nature; feelings of frustration or lostness may only increase our mistreatment of ourselves and our world.

Unhappiness often gives rise to cruel, aggressive attitudes, manipulative self-centeredness, and the need to discriminate, concretize, and control. These emotional vibrations spread through our psychological atmosphere like a toxic waste, generating more unhappiness and frustration.

*"We are losing the light
that belongs to the natural lineage
of human being"*

*Arising
out of unhappiness
and frustration, our actions
are bound to create undesirable
consequences for our selves and our
world. Buddhism calls this "negative
karma," which is ultimately the result of
ignorance. Caught up in suffering, focused
on our immediate neediness, our vision grows
very short-range; we do not even realize at first
that our actions may cause trouble for the future.*

For two hundred years or more, our society's approach to understanding nature has been basically experimental, without an enlightened and global vision. This path to knowledge has had side-effects that we did not expect, and the consequences of many of the actions already underway cannot be predicted even by our best minds.

Making decisions and acting without assurance that the future is protected lead to ever more dangerous positions, each harder to control than the last.

Our whole world begins to feel unpredictable and uncertain. Anxiety only compels us to gain control as soon as possible, without investigating the causes of the imbalances.

Pressured by complex problems, thoughts and emotions become tangled, turning increasingly negative and confused.

We struggle with ourselves, our emotions, our thoughts, but we cannot control them any more than we can control nature. The very architecture of our minds seems unstable and ungrounded.

Uncertain where to turn, depressed and lonely, people lose touch with natural human resources and become unable to care for others, for their world, or even for themselves.

We are gradually using up both our outer and inner re-sources. The human heart feels exhausted, the light of the mind seems to grow dim. Could we eventually lose the light that belongs to the natural lineage of human being?

Light is essential for our being to unfold.
Like flower petals spreading out in the sunlight,
the bud of the human heart opens to beauty,
while light transmits that beauty.

Joy, harmony, bliss, and tranquility
are available to us,
but their reflection has become very dim and unstable,
an image in a shallow, dirty lake.

Cut off from beauty and joy, our lives lose their grace and natural rhythm. Time itself seems faster and heavier, pressuring and controlling us. Inwardly we feel betrayed; human beings seem to have lost a sense of independence, as though the human spirit had been defeated by the momentum of time. Our time is already taken up by patterns and conditions dictated by society. But these patterns do not guarantee happiness or success.

A whole lifetime may not be enough time to find happiness; a whole career may not be enough time to succeed. What we have learned to call progress may actually be a process of acquisition and destruction that only depletes our resources.

If we work without satisfaction, we become mere slaves of time, imprisoned by the rationale of civilization. Breaking out of these patterns is almost unthinkable, for we might be considered crazy, outsiders, or unreliable citizens.

How easily we are caught in a downward spiral: founded on ignorance and unhealthy emotions, one misguided action leads to another and another, heading toward an unbalanced situation. Warning signals are sounded, signs are before us, inviting us to pay attention, to care, to alter our attitude. The worse the situation becomes, the more powerful the feedback becomes: the warning signals grow louder, the signs sharper and clearer.

This feedback is our opportunity for discovering a new approach if we do not allow it to overwhelm us. Often we feel that complex large-scale problems are beyond our power to comprehend, and we cannot even bear to think about them. There seems to be nothing we can do. But if we ignore them, problems only grow worse, running in vicious circles.

The pollution of the mind has given rise to the destruction of the environment, and now the unhealthy environment has become toxic to the body and mind, creating more anxiety and confusion. With so many people on the planet, we can easily damage the environment; and the consequences will be inflicted now on five billion people.

We cannot reverse what has already happened, but we could prevent negative patterns from repeating in the future if we could develop a broader and deeper perspective, a freer way of thinking. The time has come to explore the connection between the inner and outer environment, to discover the causes of our inner pollution, and to develop appreciation in the place of aggression. If we found a better way to encourage genuine healthiness and wholeness, we might find a new approach to the environment as well.

Likewise, the appreciation we develop for our natural world will help us find a more balanced, sane approach to ourselves. Treating nature with reverence and appreciation, we might learn to treat ourselves the same way.

Reverence and appreciation are fundamental to a positive way of life that develops and preserves our resources of human energy and awareness.

In place of crowdedness and tension, pollution and depression, we need a sense of spaciousness and positive accommodation, a sense of clarity and cleanness, and a feeling of inspiration.

If we face our problems directly and investigate what is restraining or pressuring us, we might begin to bring balance to our lives. No matter what direction we look, north, south, east, or west, we find problems. Yet each direction possesses its own distinctive beauty, knowledge, and strength.

If we could assemble this knowledge, share this beauty, and combine these strengths, wholesomeness could be created. Individually each one of us could emphasize more global awareness and develop a clearer understanding of the consequences of our actions.

If we took responsibility to develop harmony among all the forms of life on the planet, we could make a tremendous difference.

At the same time we would support the main purpose of our individual lives, fostering the inner growth of knowledge and the development of our potential as human beings. Developing this potential is inseparable from developing harmony on the planet and respect for all forms of life.

The Power of the Natural World

*W*alking through a garden, field or forest, we can feel our mood is shifted by the vibrant royal colors that nature presents: the greens and blues, the yellows and magentas; the lush textures and revealing forms. Expansive fields, high mountains, darkened woods have their own moods that we can share. Certain shapes and forms seem connected with distinct types of thoughts and not others.

In the presence of beauty or majesty, lonely or depressed thoughts depart, and anxiety and pressure relent. The emotions that restrain our hearts and the thoughts that pattern our mind are transformed when we are surrounded by nature.

Natural forms, shapes and colors reflect a kind of artistry that resonates with the consciousness of human beings.

The image of a flower or a bird in flight is transmitted through eye contact to our mind.

Our senses are in natural harmony with the outer world so that the external object is presented to our minds in an immediate experience of light, form, and feeling.

This form merges with and "prints" on the mind, arousing a distinct field of feeling and direction of thought.

If we notice carefully how we respond to a flower or a bird, we can almost feel the shape with our eyes; it seems there is an inner light shining within the form that harmonizes with our inner eyes.

When we pay close attention, we see vivid colors, exquisite shapes, unlimited textures and patterns, revealed in each moment of experience. We can recognize a specific feeling in each different type of locale, each different animal or plant, even in each different flower.

Sensory experiences bring the field of feeling alive, sometimes evoking memories, or different kinds of thoughts, each generating deeper levels of relaxation.

This spaciousness loosens the senses and opens the heart. Communicating with the world of nature changes consciousness.

*Beauty is here in the
midst of our world,
in the midst of our lives,
inviting us to partici-
pate and communicate.*

*This communication
can enrich our
experience and our
way of being if we
care to notice.*

*A support for our
spiritual growth,
simple natural beauty
warms the heart and
enriches the soul,
reminding us that life
is worthwhile.*

Each flower, each bird offers unique features: no two roses, and no two robins are exactly alike. An infinite exhibition of beauty is spread out before us, an unending display of patterns, shapes, and colors. Freely offered to us, this beauty touches the human heart with a gentle invitation, almost a caress.

Each individual shape and form speaks this sweet communication if we would only hear. Each one dances before us, manifesting its special qualities for our appreciation, if we would only look and see. This communication is a wonderment: It is our good fortune as human beings to be interconnected and deeply involved in this larger world. We might cherish and feel cherished in return.

"Cherishing beauty
is the secret key
to opening the heart"

*"The presence of beauty is
the beauty of presence"*

*Natural aesthetics demonstrates the nature of reality itself;
the presence of beauty is the beauty of presence. In the face
of beauty, the human heart is moved to appreciation, joy,
gratitude, and reverence.*

*When beauty resonates within us, speaking intimately to our
soul, we realize we belong to nature, and our nature belongs
to beauty. This is our refuge.*

*Beauty inseparable from love protects and opens the heart,
and stimulates the soul to grow. Natural goodness reveals
itself, witnessed by appreciation that expands and deepens.*

Let us not forget that our being has this wholesome quality too, and that our journey through life has a correspondence with beauty.

This richness of being flows in space and time, reflected in the rhythms of the seasons. We are part of this junction, part of the whole, completely involved in the process. The individual communicates directly and nakedly with beauty.

This beautiful flower is here before you, speaking, saying to you: Look, here am I. Look! And we look and that is part of us.

Something is being offered to us, and we have to look into it. See how tender is the rose.

First it seems we need to learn how to pay attention, to see, to communicate, to respond.

This spiritual way of being embraces all forms of life. Whether we are in a garden or in the wilderness, the various trees and flowers, all the plant and animal life invites us to be healthy and wholesome. We could let nature nurture us through all our senses.

We live in a garden of paradise, surrounded by beauty that is indescribable, like the beauty spoken of in the Buddhist sutras.

If we can begin to identify our own space with the vastness of space and our own form with the beauty appearing within the accommodating horizon of space, we will touch levels of experience that are richer, lighter, and more accommodating.

"Beauty is
a form of knowledge,
manifesting
the spirit of light"

This accommodation would give us room to grow and develop. Now, our inner space may feel wholly occupied with thoughts while the outer world seems already overflowing with objects. Mind and body feel tense and pressured, squeezed into too small a space too small to allow us to touch ourselves deeply.

*"The human heart thrives
on wonder and the light of beauty"*

If we do have more open experiences, we may quickly begin to interpret and lay claim to the moment. Or we may share our feelings with friends who may not wish to see us change, and we become discouraged. We may meet seekers who claim to have found "the way" and simply fall into a new belief system rather than discovering for ourselves. To enter into true inquiry and to commit to true openness take intelligence, time and energy.

We could begin a love affair with space, opening more and more room for our thoughts, expanding the field of experience.

These thoughts have been taking up all our space for years so that we miss the space itself.

We begin to notice space as the background for all forms, space as the all-pervasive openness that allows inner thoughts and outer forms to appear.

Our own sense of space can open beyond boundaries so that the whole world is totally "ours" and yet so vast that it is ungraspable.

Within this vastness there are many realms of experience, and many different realities, so we do not need to hold to a fixed model. It is more useful to stimulate knowledge.

Our body and mind already manifest tremendous knowledge, their very form and functioning beautifully integrated, elegantly patterned.

Within this body and mind there is potential for healing and knowing that can be refined and developed.

This knowledge belongs to us and this vastness is our natural realm where the human heart is nourished with wonder and the light of beauty.

Imagine that you are completely empty,
that inner space is free and unoccupied. Imagine
that gradually and gently the heart begins to open,
like a little bud of light expanding in space.

If we are willing to free our intelligence
and refine our minds, our actions will become
pure and free of mistakes. An intuitive sense of knowledge
begins to emerge, a body of knowledge arises.
We touch again the aliveness, wonder,
and simplicity of childhood;
we find our way home.

Space accommodates us,
and time can inspire us.
Yet, we are bewildered
by the steady onrush of time,
that causes us to feel helpless.

We simply participate in the flow,
carried along by the currents of time
unable to make an independent choice.

Time seems
to be speeding up
relentlessly,
each decade flying by
faster than the last.
Our calendars
are crammed full,
with no time left.

Time seems to be
"running out"
on human beings:
no time for
beauty or love,
no time for joy
or accomplishment.

To be satisfied and effective human beings,
we need the knowledge that can command time.
With intelligence we can open dimensions
in what seems to be past, present, and future.

The past must be connected
to the present and the present to the future.

So the essential quality of
time is unity rather than
separation, wholeness
rather than partitions.

If there are no differences in
the qualities of past, present, and future, then time
does not really move from
past to future—it does not
intrinsically possess
momentum.

Our reality can open to a realm where time, space, and
knowledge are undivided, without beginning or end.

Awareness can become familiar with this unity,
and contact time and space directly. Then
we begin to explore avenues towards
beautiful new realms.

Let awareness enter into each moment
in a more accurate way, and
embrace experience.

Notice a small unit of time, and then make that unit
smaller
and
smaller.

As we touch more infinitesimal portions of time, a sense of intimacy may begin to arise, leading us to different realms. These realms are filled with treasures we have been missing.

A true sense of immediacy and all-inclusive knowing comes forth, beyond language, beyond the concepts and labels that we substitute for the direct taste of experience. Free of projections and words, unpressured by time's momentum, we contact reality, our true home.

"Can we learn to see all forms of existence
as a great knowledge presenting itself?"

Mandala of Beauty

H *uman beings and this planet share five elements: water, earth, air, fire, and space. These five support all life. For example, sound communicates through space to the ears, and light to the eyes; fragrances are carried on the wind to the nose; food travels through the body via water. Senses and objects interact and merge together, objects presenting themselves to awareness through light. This interaction itself can lead to balance or imbalance, depending on how we respond to the aesthetic of nature.*

Aesthetic balance is the characteristic of the mandala. A mandala is a Buddhist model, meaning "center-periphery". It symbolizes the structure of reality in distinctive components, which together give the whole its characteristics.

Based on an ancient knowledge of universal correspondences, the mandala integrates shapes and colors with the elements and the points of the compass in a symmetrical representation of the harmony of the universe. Recognizing the mandala pattern of experience elicits the full potential of being.

The modern world has lost touch with the knowledge of the mandala, which has now become difficult to transmit and explain. But we can glimpse the principle of the mandala in art and nature: the balanced symmetry between center and surrounding field, and the wholeness inherent in beauty.

Our consciousness does respond to beautiful, balanced forms through communication with the five senses. This response itself exhibits the connectedness between the inner and outer, which is part of the communication of the mandala.

From the Buddhist point of view, the environment is a mandala, a realm of the sacred or a heavenly paradise, Sukhavati, that manifests the beauty of the Buddha nature. Entering the mandala, we embrace the embodiment of knowledge, the primordial nature of experience. The five Dhyani Buddhas symbolically represent the whole of experience: Vairocana, in the center, represents all shapes and forms

Amitabha symbolizes
desires, sensuality, and passions

Ratnasambhava
represents
feeling tones

Amoghasiddhi
represents
action and
creation

Akshobhya represents
consciousness

The elegant beauty of these Buddhas is not a veneer on the surface of experience; it is not manufactured to cover over or replace something, like a coat of colorful paint upon a gray wall. These five aspects express the unmanufactured nature of beauty itself.

According to the Tantric tradition, these five constituents of ordinary being can become the wisdom of the Buddha families. The texts describe specific techniques using meditation, mantra, visualization, and mandala to cultivate this potential. Individuals who have been properly initiated into these methods by teachers holding the Tantric lineages are readily able to transcend obstacles to freedom.

We can move in a spiritual direction by communicating with nature. The flower is a mandala form, a central point surrounded by petals in the four directions, a symbol of consciousness in space and time. The outermost petals are like past memories, the inner array like future concerns, and the center is the present where subject and object interact. From this interaction, the whole field of thoughts and associations arises in all its variety: positive, negative, and neutral thoughts, virtuous and unvirtuous thoughts.

*If we take care in the present,
then the past and future are accommodated.
Growth naturally and genuinely arises out of this caring presence,
a blossom opening in this moment.*

*In the West,
we might
say the rose
of the heart
is blooming.*

*In the East,
the lotus is a
symbol of
the Buddha
heart.*

The little bud that is the heart begins to open. The senses nourish the heart, and the opening heart stimulates the creative cognitive mind and nourishes the senses in return. Senses and mind now dynamically balance one another, and enjoyment and appreciation collect in the heart. Love flows through beauty into our being, and the heart opens wide.

This beauty is not seen by the ordinary senses; it is the quiet observant mind that can read the silent language of nature. Flowers smile upon us, and their characteristics speak inwardly to the mind and heart. We exchange gifts, like friends, and rejoice together. The flower and I communicate, the heart and mind communicate.

When mind is in one place and heart in another, we become incoherent to ourselves, and our very being feels torn with conflict and dichotomies. We no longer know who we are; we forget how to care for ourselves or for others.

When the heart is open and connected to senses and mind, balance and depth of feeling develop in ways that go beyond the ordinary operation of our embodiment. We enter a paradise realm of beauty: We embrace appearance, and appearance embraces us.

Human beings are attracted to beautiful, desirable objects, and this very desire could become a skillful means to introduce deeper appreciation for nature into our lives.

We could begin in our own backyard, creating a small garden, enjoying our favorite plants, watching each one grow. These simple plants can become friends that satisfy all our senses, offering us wonderful colors and shapes, subtle fragrances, delicious fruits and vegetables. Their substance even becomes part of our bodies, supporting our life and nourishing us like a mother.

Recognizing the motherhood of nature, we might feel reverence, appreciation, and a desire for a deeper understanding of this unique relationship.

Spending time in a garden nourishes the soul; it softens the heart and tempers harsh, unaccommodating attitudes. When we are surrounded by beautiful blossoms, it is difficult to hold on to anger and frustration or to respond to everyday pressures in the ordinary way.

Something new is introduced to consciousness; an uncrowded field or space appears where fresh memories, thoughts, and images might spring up, unfixed and unmanufactured.

The heart opens and we feel a deep connectedness that cannot be pronounced or specified exactly, a moment of childlike simplicity, wonder, and trust.

Once we recover this openness, we can encourage ourselves to open our hearts to human beings and learn to love.

*"The more we appreciate beauty
the more beauty we discover"*

*The more we appreciate beauty,
the more beauty we can discover.
Appreciation reveals new
dimensions, deepening our
experience again and again.*

*Nature's art is a mysterious
and sweet song, a song that
the human heart never tires of.
Each time we hear this melody,
we are refreshed and uplifted.*

*An elegant dance is performed to this music,
a pageant of light and color created by an artist
greater than any human genius.*

The artistry shines through
each gesture of the dance,
an expression offered
for our appreciation,
a dance performed
for our benefit.

When we walk
through a garden,
can we hear the song
being sung to the heart?

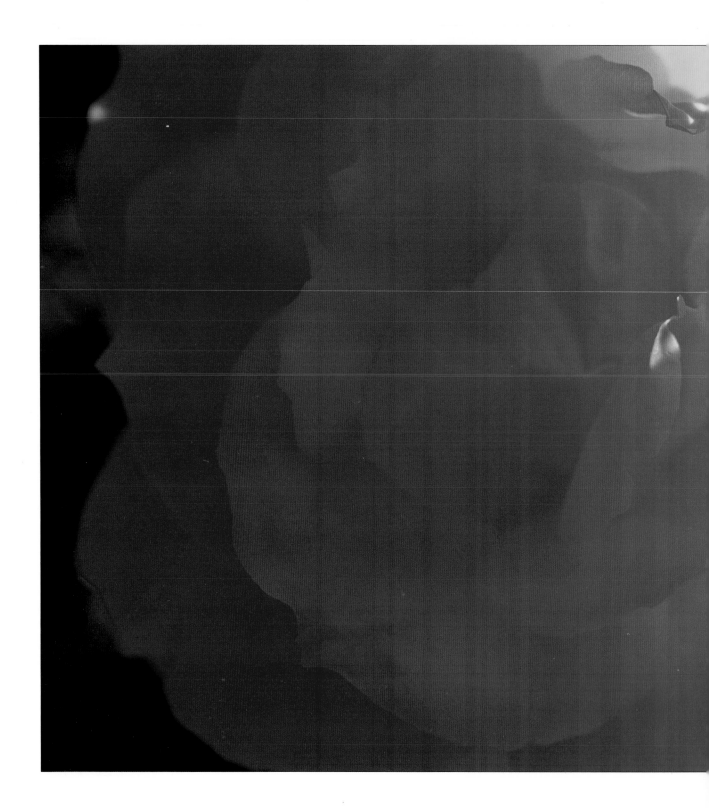

Before we met with beauty,
we did not know our soul.
Now we recognize the soul
when it responds
to the call of beauty.

The voice of beauty speaks
of the nature of the universe:
inexhaustible forms
unfolding throughout time,
beauty carries on
from age to age.

A flight of cranes
moving fearlessly
through the autumn sky
reveals the secret rhythms
of nature, knowledge deeply
in tune with time and space.

What is the mission of this beauty so freely presented
to humanity, this beauty that seems to pour forth effortlessly
into our world?

Nature's aesthetics is not in anything or of anything. Who or
what does it represent? What is this beauty attempting to do?
Has it accomplished its mission? This mystery shines
through the forms, part of the beauty itself.

The vitality of nature, the green fire of life may dwindle if it is
left untended and unacknowledged. Can we respond to it
and let it nourish us? The soul would wander in the wild
greenery of this paradise that waits in each moment for our
participation, inviting us to join the richness and embrace
the beauty.

*Is it possible that beauty exists
to enrich our soul,
to open our heart, and to expand our mind?*

These moments of beauty are bestowed upon us, like precious gifts, like rare initiations, connecting us to a spiritual path of Enlightenment.

The opening heart is the most beautiful flower of all. The greatest beauty in the world is compassion, love shining free of attachment and grasping.

Mandala of the Inner Senses

*L*earning how to take responsibility for our inner environment will make a difference for our lives and for the well-being of our planet. Our inner garden has been neglected for a long time, but the ground is fertile. With attention and care, it will bring forth delicious fruits and lovely flowers, wild greenery, and majestic trees. Once we decide to follow the way of beauty, our inner garden will never disappoint us, so rich is its potential. Every day new seeds sprout, new blossoms open, and new birds arrive.

If we want to cultivate beauty in our lives, we can use this present opportunity. Each day we can take a short time to open the senses and find a simple way to meditate. Working in this inner garden, we cultivate positive thoughts, positive imagination, and joyful feelings. When we feel discouraged, we can turn to the outer garden of nature for refreshment and nourishment.

Learning to dedicate our energy to the positive rather than the negative takes practice. But once we begin to rely on beauty, we will soon be rewarded with an abundant harvest.

Refining the Senses

The traditional design of a mandala reflects the natural harmony that exists among color, direction, and the senses. White is in the east, yellow in the south, red in the west, green in the north, and blue in the center. Seeing is associated with the east, smelling connected with the south, tasting with the west, hearing with the north, and body sensing with the center.

These five faculties and their fields of interaction express our human embodiment. Our being is naturally part of a mandala even as beginners in meditative practice. Awareness operates through the senses, each faculty expressing its own rhythm and timing, its own inner texture. Exercising these faculties begins to develop the inner side of the senses that connects us to the ground of human being. Vast and subtle levels of the senses can be developed by advanced yogic practices that work with philosophical and psychological analyses and meditative exercises.

It is not necessary, however, to know formal meditation to begin to exercise the senses. Each inner sensory faculty and outer field expresses a facet of being that we can enter into deeply. The distinctive textures and feeling tones of each of our sense can be touched, expanded, and deepened with practice. We might wish to find a beautiful spot in nature where we can sit quietly or we might prefer to walk.

Loosening the body and mind, we first relax the muscles from the top of the body down: head, neck, shoulders, arms, chest, belly, legs, and feet. Letting tensions drop away, we allow the mind to be at ease as well, unoccupied, and free of psychological or philosophical analysis.

Once completely at ease, the whole field of mind and body begins to feel different and more spacious. Now we can invite the fields of each sense to join us: vibrant colors and distinct forms, rich fragrances and tastes, subtle textures of sensations, the rhythms of sounds. As the senses come alive, we connect more intimately and deeply with experience.

For five or ten minutes, try to sustain the richness. Periodically through the day, relax deeply and open the senses for a few minutes. Extend each period of relaxation until it lasts twenty or thirty minutes. As you become more familiar with inner calm, the depth of feeling tones, and the vivid presence of experience, you will be able to tune to the subtle levels of the senses more easily. With practice, you can find your way to this realm of richness anytime you wish.

Many of us today simply do not have the time to meditate for long periods, but we can use this informal approach to good advantage: first relaxing body and calming mind, then tuning in to the senses, expanding the experience, and then deepening the feelings.

Nourishing and Protecting the Heart

As we find our way to richer realms of experience, and tune in to different levels of the senses, mind and body become more stable, more joyful, and more aware. As consciousness connects more intimately with each sensory faculty and field, we touch vastness and depth.

Without taking any position, without any conceptual instructions, we simply see. The presence of forms and eye consciousness unite beyond interpretation so there is nothing more than seeing. Letting the unknown and unfixed simply be, we sink deeper into direct experiencing.

The more deeply we sink into experience, the richer the "taste" becomes. Like a delicious fragrant nectar, the inner juice of direct experiencing flows to the heart center, nourishing our being. As heart and senses join, consciousness deepens and our being feels complete and unified.

Just as bees collect pollen and transform it into honey, we can collect the subtle levels of sense experience and refine them into nectar for the heart. The inner channels of the five senses provide a perfect food, the nectar of beauty. But the nourishing energy of beauty becomes available only if the senses operate in a more refined manner. Learning to attune ourselves to the inner side of the senses, we can begin this refinement process.

When we know how to nourish the heart, our being can unfold. Nourished and at ease, we grow stable, unified, and well balanced. Present in a beautiful realm, we exchange a deep inner appreciation with the world.

Once we are familiar with the treasures of the heart center, the inner mandala can develop. Being who we are without conceptualizing, free of interpretations, this presence does not depend on localized time, specific objects or spaces, or on memory and meanings. These are not primary to the inner mandala of our being.

Complete without depending on external conditions, we are no longer caught in the objects of the senses or lost in confusion or vagueness. Independent and present, we are free from the pressures that ordinarily control our lives, from "above or below." Doctrines and dogmas cannot oppress us; emotions and thoughts, fear and guilt can no longer control us. Our presence is alive and full of energy, oriented toward positive action.

Once we find this spiritual freedom residing in the center of the heart, we cannot be trapped in dualistic systems and interpretations. No longer involved with the "who" that is conceptually dividing experience, we are simply free and whole, balanced and independent.

Inner and Outer Balance

Wholeness is the key to inner balance, protecting us against the changing circumstances of daily life. Well-nourished and satisfied, we no longer restlessly wander in search of food for our soul. We no longer need to grasp at experience or strip the natural world bare of fruit and flowers to appease our hunger. Unswayed, unpressured, we have regained our natural balance.

When our inner environment is in balance, it begins to have effects on the outer environment. If we begin with inner balance, harmony in the outer world will develop naturally.

If we focus only on the external environment, we may miss the root of the problems; even a perfect external environment cannot guarantee a positive inner environment. No matter how beautiful the primeval forest, the animals there do not live in harmony with one another. There is an inner spiritual work required for beauty to foster balance.

When the inner environment feels unbalanced, we can tune in to the senses and allow the outer environment to nourish our hearts. Human beings have thousands of years of history shared with the planet. Our bodies and minds grew up under this sky, warmed by this sunlight, refreshed by these breezes. We can rely on an ancient partnership to help us return to our natural being.

As we reconnect head and heart and senses, inner and outer worlds, we let the harmony of the mandala guide us toward balance. Once we have found our inner balance, we can act in the outer world with confidence.

When the heart is open, satisfied, and well cared for, we feel joyful and loving toward the world. Enfolded in the heart of natural being, loneliness and confusion disappear.

The senses come alive, awareness is present, intelligence and good judgment are active. Without struggling with ourselves, we feel compassion arising naturally. Though we may have causes worth fighting for, we find we get better results in an easier, more accommodating way. The positive harmonious quality of open-hearted action manifests.

If we maintain this inner balance, we will find ways to accommodate nature and protect the environment. We know our interactions with the world of nature must be properly balanced or serious consequences will follow; choices we make today may have far-ranging effects in the future. As we become more aware of this partnership with the earth, we see that balance is critical.

Balance begins with each of us. If individuals take responsibility for their own inner environment and learn how to nourish the heart, human activity will grow less destructive to our own species and to the planet.

Taking care of ourselves only seems selfish, for once we know how to do this, we can easily overcome real selfishness. If we cannot make the heart genuinely happy, we have little to offer and little capacity for selfless action.

There is no need to wait to take care of ourselves. We cannot predict how much time we will have to cultivate this inner garden, so we ought to begin today to follow the way of beauty. Each morning we can chose three positive thoughts to strengthen. At the same time we can forgive ourselves completely and let go of negative ways of thinking, guilt, and self-discouragement.

Gradually we will see improvement. It is vitally important to fill the heart with the enjoyment of positive actions rather than the discouragement of endless problems. Instead of being entangled in thoughts and emotions, our energy flows freely, fully alive. Refreshing this aliveness, stimulating it, and encouraging it, we sustain a meaningful way of life. Even if we do not reach great heights of spiritual accomplishment, we will live with integrity, ease, and contentment.

When we take responsibility to stop polluting our own heart and mind with negativity, confusion, and divisiveness, we begin to create something of great value not only for ourselves, but for others and eventually for the entire planet. Once we touch the inner beauty of being and realize its great value, we recognize our duty to protect it.

A positive attitude shining through our life becomes an exhibition of grace and beauty that touches others, communicating directly to the heart. Rich enough to share freely with others, we can support our families and friends as they learn to gain their balance. As the roses bloom in our inner garden, we offer the fragrance and beauty back to the world.

Healing our own souls will empower us to heal the planet. We know that wholesome and compassionate attitudes spread from person to person. Our individual positive experience may seem a tiny point in the vast network of the planet. But from that point radiate ever-widening circles of influence, the power of peaceful joy, compassion, and love.

Odiyan Mandala

S *ince arriving in America in 1969, Tarthang Tulku had envisioned a country center that would accommodate a wide range of activities including traditional Buddhist studies, research, and practice, sacred art projects, preservation of Tibetan culture, and a meeting ground for Eastern and Western forms of knowledge.*

To locate the land, many trips were made for several years throughout northern California. Suitable property was located in 1974, 108 miles northwest of Rinpoche's center in Berkeley. The land reminded him of Oddiyana, the kingdom northwest of India, and the birthplace of Padmasambhava, the great master who brought Buddhism to Tibet in the 8th century. It was only later that Rinpoche discovered that the ancient Oddiyana is directly on the opposite side of the globe from the modern Odiyan.

The Odiyan land consists of over a thousand acres, with forested ridges unfolding as though they were petals of a lotus. Two rivers flow on either side of the property, reminiscent of the diagrams of yin and yang energies in the human body.

The land had been used for generations as a sheep ranch, and the hills had been logged extensively. Before that time, the ridges had been holy ground to the Pomo Indians, this particular location known as Crest of the Condor. In the spring of 1975 architectural planning was well underway, and by August 9 the land was consecrated in a special ceremony and named Odiyan in honor of the kingdom of Oddiyana.

Odiyan was designed by Tarthang Tulku as a mandala, a dynamic ordered arrangement of forms, a pattern that embodies creative action. The fundamental structure is an inner space surrounded by elements placed in the four directions. Associated with each direction are colors, shapes, elements, and symbols of the human body and mind, and the larger cosmos. Many Tibetan paintings reflect this mandala structure.

Architecture based on a mandala pattern is more complex. Samye, the first Buddhist temple in Tibet, was constructed as a mandala. Creating a mandala is a very meaningful endeavor spiritually and psychologically, establishing a pattern for refining human nature and eliciting authenticity.

Such an undertaking was quite a challenge for a small group of new Dharma students with a single teacher, and a number of friends and advisors recommended against it. Nonetheless, in 1975 volunteers renovated the old farmhouse on the property which served as housing for the crew of workers. They next began the task of cleaning up the land, removing hundreds of damaged and rotten trees and tree stumps from hill after hill.

For three years, land was cleared and trees pruned, and then reforesting work was begun in cooperation with the California Department of Forestry. Each year we added many thousands of one- and two-year old bare-root seedlings of Douglas firs, ponderosa pines, Afghan pines, coast redwoods, and incense cedars.

Over a hundred thousand forest trees have been planted, and they can be seen growing everywhere on the land. We have also planted many varieties of flowering trees and shrubs, and thousands of fruit trees in six orchards. Over the last twelve years, these young seedlings and plants have made an astonishing difference in the land.

In 1976, water was located on the land, and a well was dug, giving Odiyan over 90 gallons per minute of flow. For two generations the former owners had tried to locate a well no avail, and they lost hope of farming or irrigating the land.

We still do not understand our good fortune, but today three enormous wells exist while neighboring pieces of land still struggle with no water. A geologist who visited Odiyan found an underground formation that he described as heart-shaped with many veins and rivulets of water. No one knows where this water comes from.

In 1977 the initial rim structure was completed, including 50 residential rooms, kitchen, libraries, meeting rooms. In 1980 the Odiyan Enlightenment Stupa was constructed, a traditional Buddhist monument that promotes natural harmony. The main temple was completed thereafter, followed by several years of continuing projects focused on ornamentation.

In 1984 excavation was begun to create a lake around the temple complex. That same year, several thousand silver plates were added to the face of the Stupa. In 1986 the Odiyan statue project completed seventy-five life-size statues for the Temple and Stupa, while the surface of the Stupa was refinished in gold.

In 1986 extensive plans for the Odiyan gardens were being developed. The four sides of the temple complex, the area around the Stupa, and the gardens around the farmhouse would each manifest distinctive qualities. Much time, effort, and money has been spent over the years refining these gardens, improving the soil, and adding irrigation systems.

Many exotic plants from around the world have been added to the Odiyan gardens. We have been particularly happy to discover that rare magnolias and rhododendrons from Asia can flourish in this climate when given appreciative attention.

In 1988 the World Peace Garden was developed around the Enlightenment Stupa. The orchards were expanded, and another 50,000 trees added to the property in a reforestation effort.

Gradually, the entire property becomes part of the mandala, the areas closest to the temple the most cultivated, the more distant regions remaining wild but cared for. In 1988 a pathway around the entire property was created, a long pilgrimage walk that takes the visitor to all the special areas of Odiyan, such as Vairotsana Hill, Lavender Hill, and Tibetan Hill.

One hundred and eight small stupas were erected in carefully chosen locations all around the land. Each region has a distinctive quality and energy that directly affects consciousness. Some places are quietly reflective; others are challenging and stimulating; some evoke deep and subtle feelings and sensations. Walking across the land, spending time in different locations, we learn a great deal about human nature and nature at large.

The mandala includes the pattern made by the rhythms of time as well as the directions in space. Each period of time, each season at Odiyan is distinctive. Like a playful spirit, Odiyan changes by the hour, its colors and moods shifting dramatically. Morning brings a misty mysterious quietness; noontime is dynamic and brilliant; sunset is luxurious and restful; and midnight is vast and open, with starry skies close enough to touch. Nature at Odiyan speaks very loudly and clearly. The space is immense, the sky always present to consciousness. Rainbows and unusual lights appear frequently. Sunlight sparkles on the lake, the copper roofs, and the golden Stupa.

Odiyan communicates to us, a precious wordless teaching in the language of the heart. Without being told, without being preached to, we learn naturally. Beauty is so powerful at Odiyan it is almost overwhelming. It beckons to us every day in vivid colors, elegant shapes, and inspiring vistas. Touching our consciousness, uplifting our moods, balancing our energies, Odiyan is a living embodiment of the Buddhist teachings, a mandala of wisdom and compassion.

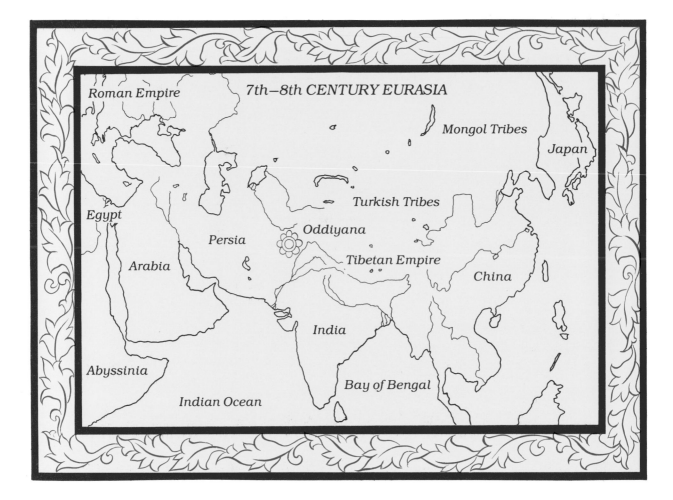

7th–8th CENTURY EURASIA

Roman Empire

Mongol Tribes

Japan

Turkish Tribes

Egypt

Persia

Oddiyana

Tibetan Empire

Arabia

China

India

Abyssinia

Bay of Bengal

Indian Ocean

The Kingdom of Oddiyana
Land of the Lineage of Diamond Light

 *The Kingdom of Oddiyana*

*T*he kingdom of Oddiyana has been identified by modern scholars as the modern Swat Valley in the mountain ranges of the northwestern corner of the Indian subcontinent. Just to the south, the ancient Indus Valley civilization rose and fell thousands of years ago.

To the east is found the old kingdom of Kashmir, and farther east, across the Himalayas stretches the plateau of Tibet. To the north, the Silk Road linked the central Asian kingdoms together and connected China to Rome. The routes running east from Oddiyana traveled through the Persian empire and the ancient land of Mesopotamia to Egypt.

According to the classical Buddhist histories, Oddiyana was a very important kingdom where many Tantras were preserved. There were said to be vast libraries filled with esoteric texts that masters of the yogic traditions bestowed upon the world at the proper time and place.

Other sources explain that Oddiyana was a mystical center, a sacred place of power where the blessings of the Enlightened Ones brought forth the deepest teachings on the perfection of human existence.

Odiyan Mandala Map

Legend

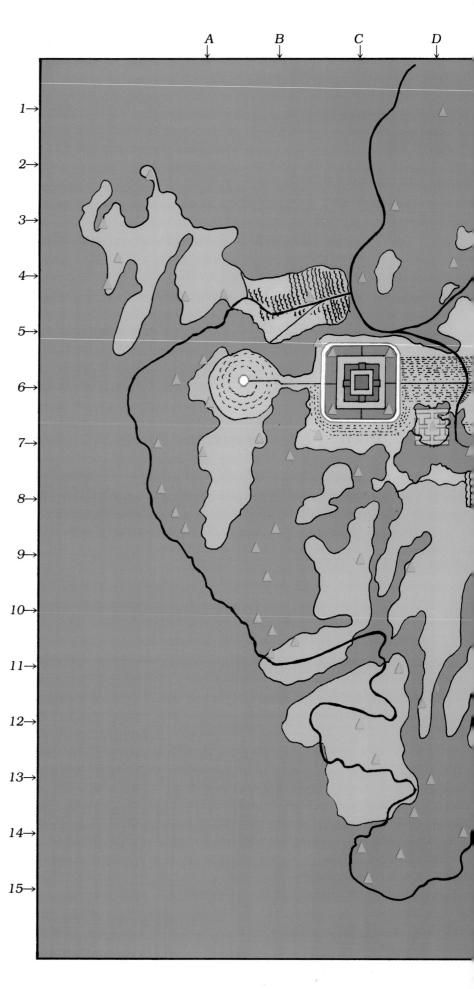

B : 8   *Douglas fir reforestation*

H : 14   *Jeffrey pine reforestation*

G : 9   *Arizona cypress reforestation*

F : 5-8   *Coast redwood reforestation*

C : 10   *Ponderosa pine reforestation*

D-H : 13   *Coast redwood reforestation*

I : 11-15   *Ponderosa pine reforestation*

D-E : 11-12   *Afghan and Aleppo pine reforestation*

D : 4   *Coast redwood reforestation*

A : 3-9   *Incense cedar reforestation*

B : 5   *Asian pear orchards*

B : 4   *Vegetable garden*

G : 7   *Pilgrimage Road*

F : 14   *Pilgrimage Road*

A : 10   *Pilgrimage Road*

C : 2   *Public road*

I : 6   *Public road*

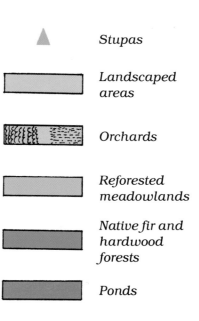

Stupas

Landscaped areas

Orchards

Reforested meadowlands

Native fir and hardwood forests

Ponds

*Overview
of
Odiyan
Temple
Grounds
and
Mandala
Garden*

Entering the Temple Grounds

At the outer edge of the pond, the Lombardy poplars have turned butter yellow, the tall Serbian spruces are dark green, and the canopy of wisteria is gold against green leaves. We are greeted by ranks of tall masts bearing colorful prayer flags high above the flaming, crimson maple trees.

Walking across a wooden bridge over the pond, we approach the rim structure of the Odiyan Main Temple. The inner edge of the pond is lined with rusty red rock, beyond which stretch strips of lawn, rows of flowering shrubs, banks of birches, all forming parallel lines that express the outflowing energy of the mandala.

The massive open doors of the entryway invite us into a darkened passage that opens to infinite shades of color and light: yellow pillars, red tile walkways, bamboo hedges give way to the space of soft lawns. A rising slope of dark green ivy climbs up ornamental fences to the top of the temple mound. Maples, cypresses, and snowbell trees flank the marble steps up to the central gardens, where the temple awaits us: the deep red of polished granite, the shining copper of the roofs suspended in an azure sky: the space of our heart filled with the rich colors of experience.

A panoramic view displays forests and mountains to the North; orchards and the Pacific Ocean to the South; the intrepid solidity of the Vajra Temple to the West, the cherry orchard and the Enlightenment Stupa to the East.

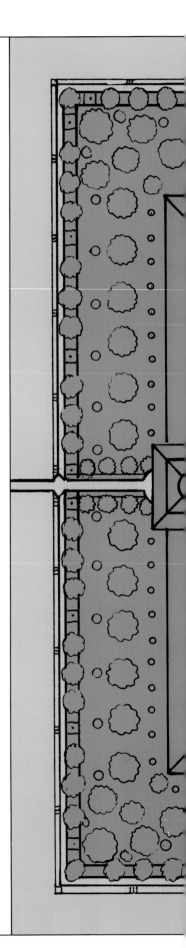

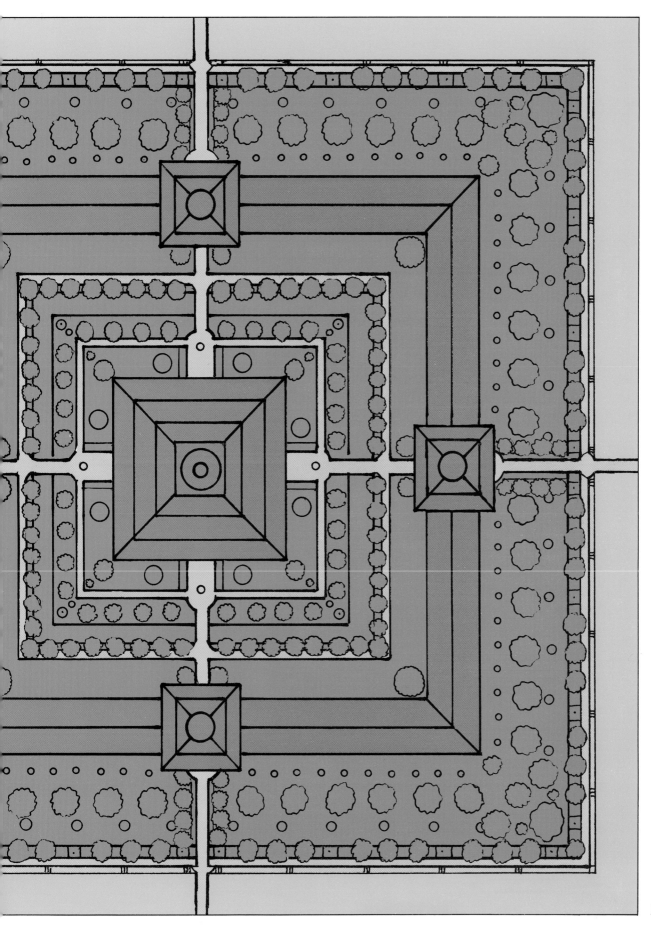

The Mandala Garden

The Mandala Garden is a mandala of plants, the well-spring of the gardens all over Odiyan. As it grows, it will become a palace of living things, with all the hues, forms, fragrances, transparencies, lights, textures, and qualities of space that are the gift of a living land.

Within this mandala we can recognize various orders. The first order is formed by a canopy of trees, up to 100 feet from the garden floor. It is made up primarily of Douglas firs, together with ancient tan oaks with silver leaves, long yellow blossoms of chestnuts, and pepperwood, known as California Bay. These trees are shown as a drift of green clouds in the drawing. Together they are the dominant, delicate, protective grace of nature.

The second order is formed by the artful design of the garden on the forest floor. At its heart is a small stupa. Here is a mandala with walks and courtyards, special spaces with walls made of rhododendrons, hallways whose windows are flowering branches.

The garden beds seem like a maze filled with roses, azaleas, lilies, and perennials of all kinds; and the younger trees: scarlet oaks, golden rhobenias, flowering apples, katsura, dogwoods, redwoods, stewartia, and magnolias with bursting blossoms.

Most of the trees have been placed like courtiers within spaces. Others seem to be moving about and can surprise you by being right in the middle of the path. From a distance these trees may become green and golden clouds, or columns that can lift your eyes to dissolve in greater translucent vaults of light and tree light. The order of these beds seems to provide us with pathways: ways to walk, sequences to notice, ways to be. This symmetry is formed by the intellect.

Finally, there is a more universal symmetry. The mandala gardens seem to be a grid with intersecting lines, interspersed with rhododendrons. There are about 200 varieties of rhododendrons in the Mandala Garden, and they are everywhere, stretching beyond to other forest gardens.

When one is captivated by the beauty of one rhododendron, at that moment it is the center of the whole garden. Each flower, although unique in itself, is like every other, and yet each one by itself is the center of all others.

Enlightenment Stupa Gardens Overview

1 : B–Y	Asian pear orchard, shrub roses
1–16 : W–Y	Plum orchard
3–15 : C–D	Cupressus pisifera 'Boulevard'
3–17 : D	Formal rose beds
3–17 : G	Incense cedars, continuing as indicated around the Stupa
4–6 : S–U	Viewing deck
4 : F	Magnolia 'Leonard Messel'
4 : H–S	'Olympiad' tree roses with 'Nevada' roses with Lingustum japonica 'Texanum' hedge behind these, continuing around the Stupa
4.5 : H–U	Concrete walkway around the Stupa
5 : G–T	Italian cypress; understory of miniature roses, perennials, and annuals; wisteria, climbing roses 'America' and 'Peace', Jasminum polyanthemum against wall
5.5 : I–T	Enclosed walkway
5.75 : I–T	Bed beneath roof overhang with roses and perennials
6 : J and R	Acer palmatum
6 : N	Magnolia denudata
6 : L	Lawn area
6.75 : K–R	Raised bed with miniature roses
7 : F	Lawn area with massed paperwhite narcissus
7 : K–R	Walkway of paving brick
7 : K and R	Standing lanterns
7.5 : O	Formal flower bed
8–12 : A	Formal rose beds
13 : L	Alberta spruce
13 : Q	Specimen laceleaf palmatum
13.5 : O	Walkway
14.5 : J–S	Rhododendrons under walkway roof overhang, this side only
15 : O	Gatehouse
16 : O	Lions at either side of door
16–18 : A	Formal rose bed; beginning of Peace Garden
17 : O	Bench
20 : O	Overstory of Douglas fir

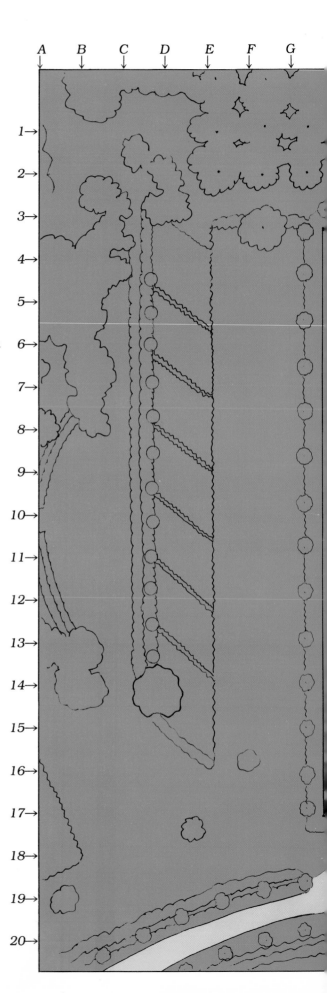

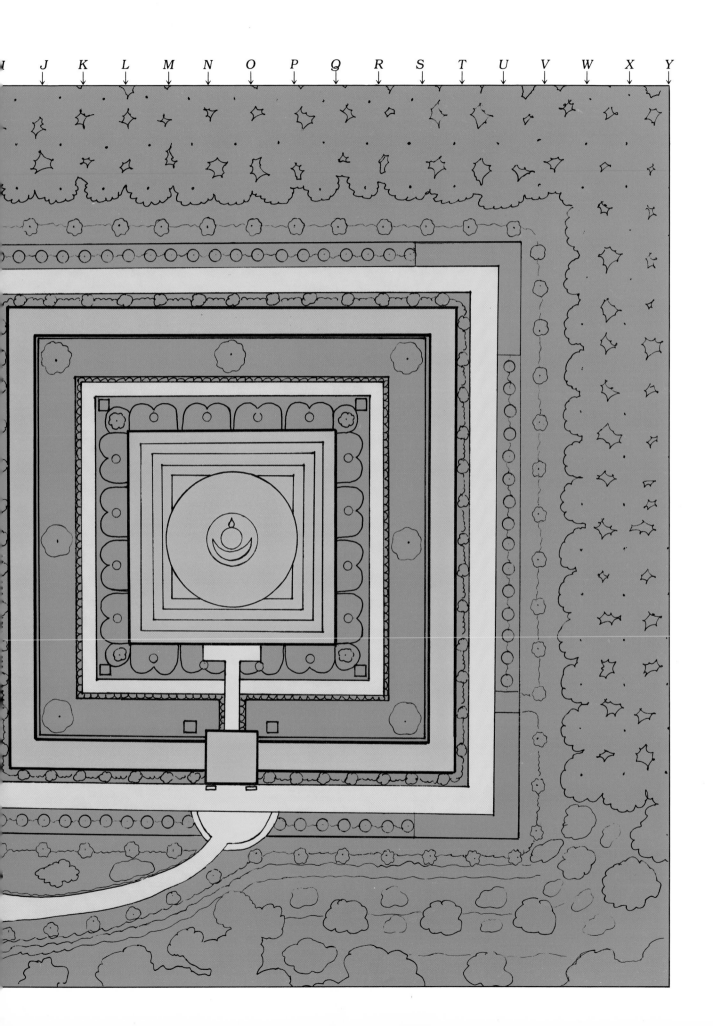

List of Major Trees and Shrubs

Abelia grandiflora 'Edward Goucher'

Abies concolor grandis

Abutilon hybridum

Acacia baileyana

Acacia 'purpurea'

Acanthus mollis

Acer buergeranum

Acer capillipes

Acer ginnala

Acer griseum

Acer japonicum 'aconitifolium', 'Maiku Jaku', 'Junihitoye', 'Kinkakure', 'O Isame'

Acer macrophyllum

Acer palmatum 'shigitatsu sawa', 'Atropurpurea', 'Atropurpurea' dissectum, 'Ayoyagi', 'Bene Schichihenge', 'Bene Otake', 'Bloodgood', 'Butterfly', 'Crimson Queen', 'Ever Red', 'Filigree', 'Garnet', 'Higasayama', 'Kasagiyama', 'Kiyohime', 'Okushimo', 'Omurayama', 'Orido Nishiki', 'Red Select', 'Sagara Nishiki', 'Sango

Kaku', 'Seiryu', 'Seikimori', 'Shindeshojo', 'Shishigashira', 'Tana', 'Trompenburg', 'Viridis' dissectum, 'Waterfall', seedlings of palmatums

Acer pentaphyllum

Acer shirasawanum 'Palmatifolium'

Acer pseudoplatanus 'Spaethii'

Acer rubrum

Acer saccharinum

Aesculus californicum

Agonis flexuosa

Albizia julibrissin

Almond 'Ne Plus Ultra', 'Non Pariel'

Alnus cordatra

Apple 'Arkansas Black orchards', 'Ashmead's Kernel', 'Black Twig', 'Bramley's Seedling', 'Calville Blanc de Hive', 'Cox Orange Pippin', 'Fuji', 'Gala', 'Golden Delicious', 'Granny Smith', 'Graven', 'Idared', 'Jonagold', 'Liberty', 'Macoun', 'McIntosh', 'Mutsu', 'Newton Pippin', 'Northern Spy', 'Pink Pearl', 'Red Delicious', 'Rome Beauty', 'Sierra Beauty', 'Spitzenberg', 'Stayman Winesap', 'Wagener', 'Winter Banana', 'Yellow Bellflower'

Apricot 'Autumn Royal', 'Sweet Kernel', 'Moorpark', 'Royal Blenheim'

Aralia elata

Araucaria araucana

Araucaria heterophylla

Arbutus menziesii

Arbutus unedo 'Compacta'

Arcotostaphylos manzanita

Aucuba 'Crotonifolia', 'Fructo Alba'

Bambusa multiplex, 'Alphonse Karr'

Berberis darwinii

Berberis thunbergii 'Atropurpurea', 'Rose Glow'

Bergenia hybrids

Betula maximowicziana

Betula pendula

Bilbergia nutans

Buddleia davidii

Buxus microphylla japonica 'Green Beauty'

Buxus sempervierens 'Arborescens', 'Aureo-variegata'

Cactaceae and aloes

Callicarpa bodieneri giraldii

Calluna vulgaris, 'Robert Chapman', 'Silver Queen'

Calocedrus decurrens

Camellia japonica cultivars

Camellia sasanqua 'Cleopatra', cultivars

Castanea dentata x mollisima

Casuarina

Ceanothus 'Blue Jeans', 'Concha', 'Frosty Blue', 'Julia Phelps', 'Ray Hartman', 'Snow Flurry'

Cedrus atlantica 'Glauca', 'Glauca pendula'

Cedrus deodara, 'Cream Puff', 'Descanso Dwarf'

Cercidiphyllum japonicum

Cercis canadensis, 'Forest Pansy'

Cercis chinensis

Cercis occidentalis

Cercis reniformis 'Oklahoma'

Chaenomeles species, 'Jet Trail', 'Tall Red', 'Toyo Nishiki'

Chamaecyparis lawsoniana 'Elwoodii Improved'

Chamaecyparis 'Grandi'

Chamaecyparis 'Nidiformis'

Chamaecyparis obtusa 'Gracilis', 'Graciosa', 'Kosteri', 'Nana Lutea', 'Sanderi', 'Wells Special'

Chamaecyparis pisifera 'Boulevard', 'Filifera Nana Aurea', 'Snow', 'Squarrosa Intermedia', 'Squarrosa Veichii'

Cherry 'Bing','Lambert', 'Montmorency', 'Rainier', 'Royal Ann', 'Sam','Stella', 'Van'

Chimonanthus praecox

Choisya ternata

Cistus hybridus

Cistus salvifolius

Cistus skanbergii

Citrus 'Owari Satsuma'

Citrus 'Valencia'

Clematis montana 'Rubens'

Clianthus puniceus

Cornus capitata

Cornus controversa

Cornus florida

Cornus kousa 'Koreana'

Cornus stolonifera 'Baileyii'

Corylus colurna

Corylus maxima

Cotinus coggygria 'Purpureus'

Cotoneaster horizontalis

Cotoneaster perpusilla 'Variegatus'

Cotoneaster salicifolia

Crataegus phaenopyrum

Cryptomeria japonica 'Elegans compacta', 'Lobbi Nana', 'Nana', seedlings

Cupressocyparis leylandii 'Castlewellan'

Cupressus glabra

Cupressus macrocarpa

Cupressus sempervirens

Cytisus kewensis

Cytisus lydia

Cytisus scopoarius

Daboecia cantabrica 'Alba'

Daphne odora 'Marginata'

Eleagnus pungens 'Maculata'

Enkianthus campanulatus

Erica carnea 'Aurea', 'Foxhollow', 'King George', 'Myretoun Ruby', 'Springwood Pink', 'Springwood White', 'Vivelli'

Erica darleyensis 'Arthur Johnson'

Erica tetralix 'Alba Mollis'

Erica vagans 'Mrs. D.F. Maxwell'

Erica watsonii 'Dawn'

Eriobotrya deflexa

Eriobotrya japonica

Escallonia exoniensis 'Fradesii'

Eucalyptus polyanthemos

Euonymus fortunei 'Kewensis'

Euryops pectinatus

Feijoa sellowiana

Felicia amelloides

Fig 'Brown Turkey', 'Genoa', 'Kadota', 'Osborne Prolific'

Forsythia intermedia

Fothergilla monticola

Fraxinus oxycarpa 'Raywood'

Fremontodendron

Fuchsia triphylla 'Gartenmeister Bonstedt'

Genista lydia

Ginko biloba 'Autumn Gold'

Hebe 'Veronica Lake'

Hedera helix 'Needlepoint'

Heteromeles arbutifolia

Hydrangea macrophylla

Hydrangea quercifolia

Hypericum 'Hidcote'

Ilex crenata 'Dwarf Pagoda', 'Green Dragon'

Juglans nigra

Juniperus chinensis 'Old Gold', 'Pfitzeriana Aurea', 'Sea Green', 'Spearmint', 'Torulosa'

Juniperus conferta 'Emerald Sea'

Juniperus horizontalis 'Blue Mat', 'Douglasii', 'Filicinus Minimus', 'Prince of Wales', 'Wiltoni'

Juniperus sabina 'Arcadia', 'Buffalo', 'Tamariscifolia New Blue'

Juniperus scopulorum 'Moonglow'

Juniperus squamata 'Blue Star'

Juniperus virginiana 'Grey Owl', 'Skyrocket'

Koelreuteria paniculata

Larix kaempferi

Lavendula angustifolia 'Hidcote'

Lavendula stoechas

Leucothoe Fontanesiana 'Rainbow'

Ligustrum japonicum 'Texanum'

Liquidambar styraciflua 'Burgandy', 'Festival', seedling, 'Palo Alto'

Lirodendron tulipfera

Lithocarpus densiflorus

Loropetalum chinense

Magnolia 'Caerhays Belle'

Magnolia cylindrica

Magnolia denudata

Magnolia 'Galaxy'

Magnolia grandiflora 'Sammuel Somer'

Magnolia 'Iolanthe'

Magnolia Kosar and De Vos hybrids 'Ann', 'Betty', 'Susan'

Magnolia liliflora

Magnolia loebneri 'Ballerina', 'Leonard Messel'

Magnolia 'Picture'

Magnolia salicifolia 'Miss Jack'

Magnolia 'Serenity'

Magnolia soulangiana seedlings

Magnolia 'Spectrum'

Magnolia springeri 'Diva'

Magnolia 'Star Wars'

Magnolia stellata 'Centennial', 'Royal Star','Waterlilly'

Magnolia 'Wada's Memory'

Magnolia wilsoni 'Bovee'

Malus 'Dolgo', floribunda, 'Hopa', ioensis 'Plena' (Bechtel), 'Oekomomierat Echtermeyer', 'Pink Spires', 'Radiant', 'Red Silver', 'Royalty', 'Silver Chalice', zumi calocarpa, alba, nigra

Myrica californica

Nandina domestica seedlings, cultivars

Nyssa sylvatica

Olea europea

Paeonia suffricosa cultivars

Parrotia persica

Peach cultivars

Pear 'Bartlett', 'California', 'Comice', 'Max Red Bartlett'

Pear (Asian cultivars) 'Chojuro', 'Hosui', 'Kikusui', 'Nijiseiki', 'Shinko', 'Shinseiki'

Pernettya mucronata

Persimmon 'Chocolate', 'Fuyu', 'Giant Fuyu', 'Hachiya'

Philadelphus virginalis

Photinia fraseri

Picea abies 'Nidiformis'

Picea brewerana

Picea glauca 'conica' (dwarf Alberta)

Picea omorica

Picea pungens 'Hoopsi', 'Montgomery'

Pieris forestii 'Bright Red'

Pieris japonica 'Variegata'

Pinus aristata

Pinus attenuata

Pinus coulteri

Pinus densiflora 'Umbraculifera'

Pinus eldarica

Pinus halapensis, 'Brutia'

Pinus jeffreyi

Pinus lambertiana

Pinus mugo

Pinus muricata

Pinus ponderosa

Pinus ponderosa x jeffreyi

Pinus radiata

Pinus thunbergiana

Pinus torreyana

Pinus wallichiana

Pistacia chinensis

Pittosporum eugenioides

Platanus acerifolia 'Bloodgood'

Plum 'Elephant Heart', 'Green Gage', 'Late Santa Rosa', 'Santa Rosa'

Populus nigra 'Italica'

Potentilla fruiticosa 'Abbottswood', 'Hollandia Gold', 'Primrose Beauty'

Prune 'Early French', 'Italian', 'Sugar'

Prunus ilicifolia

Prunus serrulata (flowering cherry) 'Kwanzan', 'Shirofugen', 'Royal Burgandy', 'Shogetsu', 'Taiwan'

Prunus subhirtella (flowering cherry), double pink,

single pink, white

Prunus cerasifera (flowering plum) 'Krauter Vesuvius'

Pseudotsuga menziesii

Pterocarya fraxinifolia

Punica granatum 'Wonderful'

Pyracantha 'Mohave'

Pyrus calleryana 'Bradford', 'Capital', 'Redspire'

Pyrus kawakamii

Pyrus salicifolia 'Pendula'

Quercus crysolepsis

Quercus coccinea

Quercus kelloggii

Quercus rubra

Quercus wislizenii

Quince fruiting 'Orange', fruiting 'Pineapple'

Raspberry hybrids

Rhododendron hybrid 'Alice Bedford', 'America', 'Anah Krushke', 'Anna', 'Anna Rose Whitney', 'Antoon van Welie', 'Autumn Gold', 'Belle Heller', 'Bill Massey', 'Black Prince', 'Blue Diamond', 'Blue Jay', 'Blue Peter', 'Blue Rhapsody', 'Bow Bells', 'Bread and Butter', 'California Blue', 'Chinoides', 'Christmas Cheer', 'Confection', 'County of York', 'Crest', 'Cynthia', 'Dame Nellie Melba', 'Dancing', 'Lady', 'Daphnoides', 'Dora Amateis', 'Dr. Arnold W. Endtz', 'Dr. Bloch', 'El Camino', 'Elizabeth Red Foliage', 'Roseum', 'Eureka

Maid', 'Everestianum', 'Fatuosum Flore Pleno', 'Fort Bragg Glow', 'Full Moon', 'Furnivall's Daughter', 'Gartendirektor Glocker', 'Goldsworth Crimson', 'Gomer Waterer', 'Graf Zepplin', 'Halfdan Lem', 'Hardijzer's Beauty', 'Ice Cube', 'Inheritance', 'Jean Marie de Montague', 'Jim Drewery', 'John Coutts', 'Johnny Bender', 'Kluis Sensatiion', 'Lady Clementine Mitford', 'Lady de Rothschild', 'Lee's Dark Purple', 'Lem's 45', 'Loder's White', 'Loderi Game Chick', 'Lord Roberts', 'Marchoness of Lansdowne', 'Margaret Mack', 'Markeeta's Flame', 'Markeetwa's Prize', 'Mary Fleming', 'Molly Ann', 'Mother of Pearl', 'Mrs. Betty Robertson', 'Mrs. Charles E. Pearson', 'Mrs. G. W. Leak', 'Mrs. J. G. Millais', 'Mrs. T. H. Lowinsky', 'Noyo Brave', 'Noyo Chief', 'Ooh Gina', 'Paprika Spiced', 'Pepperpot', 'Phyllis Korn', 'Pink Delight', 'Pinkl Pearl', 'Pink Walloper', 'P.J.M.', 'Point Defiance', 'Praecox', 'Prairie Fire', 'President Roosevelt', 'Puget Sound', 'Purple Splendor', 'Radium', 'Red Eye', 'Red Olympia', 'Rocket', 'Roseum Elegans', 'Rosy Dream', 'Royal Purple', 'Rubicon', 'Ruby Bowman', 'Sabrina Alder', 'Sappho', 'Scarlet

Wonder', 'Scintillation', 'September Song', 'Seta', 'Snow Lady', 'Spitfire', 'Taurus', 'Travis L.', 'Trilby', 'Trude Webster', 'Umpqua Chief', 'Unique', 'Virgo', 'Vulcan', 'Vulcan's Flame', 'Walloper "D"', 'White Swan', 'Yellow Hammer'

Rhododendron maddenii hybrids 'Actress', 'Alice Eastwood', 'Bill Massey', 'Butterhorn', 'California Gold', 'Conchita', 'Countess of Haddington', 'Eldorado', 'Else Frye', 'Fosterianum', 'Heaven Scent', 'Lake Lorraine', 'Lemon Mist', 'Meadowgold', 'Mi Amor', 'My Lady', 'Muriel Giaque', 'Mysterious Maddenii', 'Rose Scott', 'Sabrina Alder', 'Saffron Prince', 'Scott Maddenii', 'Scott's Valentine'

Rhododendron augustinii, Barto Blue form

Rhododendron catawbiense 'Album'

Rhododendron 'Boursault'

Rhododendron cubittii

Rhododendron formosum

Rhododendron kiusianum

Rhododendron maddenii g. langois

Rhododendron odoriferum

Rhododendron oreotrephies

Rhododendron ponticum dark form, light form

Rhododendron taronense

Rhododendron vietchianum

Rhododendron yakushimanum 'Ken Janeck', 'Phetteplace (tall form)', 'Yaku Angel'

Rhododendron (evergreen Azaleas) 'Alaska', 'Ama Gasa', 'Beni Kirishima', 'Blue Danube', 'Brilliant', 'Buccaneer', 'Caroline Gable', 'Casablanca', 'Dorothy Gish', 'Double Beauty',

'Duc de Rohan', 'Eikan', 'Everest', 'Fielder's White', 'Flame Creeper', 'Formosa' (Phoenecia), 'Geisha Girl', 'George Lindley Taber', 'Glacier', 'Glamour', 'Glory of Sunninghill', 'Gumpo Pink', 'Gumpo White', 'Hahn's Red', 'Helen Close', 'Hexe', 'Higasa', 'Hino-crimson', 'Hinodegiri', 'Kaempo', 'Louise Gable', 'Macrantha', 'Martha Hitchcock', 'Mother's Day', 'Mucronatum', 'Murasaki Shikibu', 'Osakazuki' ('Macrantha'), 'Polypetalum', 'Pride of Dorking', 'Puple Splendor', 'Redwing', 'Rosaflora', 'Rosebud', 'Rukizon', 'Sakuragata', 'Sherwood Red', 'Sherwood Orchid', 'Shinnyo no Tsuki', 'Snow Mound', 'Southern Charm', 'Stewartsonian', 'Vuyk's Rosy Red', 'Vuyk's Scarlet', 'Ward's Ruby'

Rhodendron (deciduous Azaleas)

Ribes sanguineum 'King Edward VII'

Ribes speciosum

Robinia pseudoaccacia 'Frisia'

Romneya coulteri

Rosa hybrid 'Alleluia', 'Alspice', 'America', 'Angel Face', 'Aquarius', 'Betty Prior', 'Bewitched', 'Bloomin' Easy', 'Blue Girl', 'Blue Nile', 'Brandy', 'Century Two', 'Charisma', 'Charlotte Armstrong', 'Cherry Vanilla', 'Chicago Peace', 'China Doll', 'Chrysler Imperial', 'Circus Parade', 'Confetti', 'Dolly Parton', 'Don Juan', 'Dortmund', 'Double Delight', 'Duet', 'Electron', 'Europeana', 'First Edition', 'First Prize', 'Fragrant Cloud', 'Fred Emunds', 'French Lace', 'Fruehlingsgold', 'Garden Party', 'Galway Bay', 'Gingersnap', 'Glorie de Dijon', 'Gold Medal', 'Golden Showers', 'Graceland', 'Grootendorst Supreme', 'Hansa', 'Handel', 'Helen Traubel', 'Holy Toledo', 'Honor', 'Iceberg', 'Impatient', 'Intrigue', 'Ivory Tower', 'John F. Kennedy', 'Kentucky Derby', 'Kordes Perfecta', 'Lady X', 'Lemon Spice', 'Madame Alfred Carriere', 'Margo Koster', 'Micado', 'Mirandy', 'Miss All-American Beauty', 'Miss Liberte', 'Mojave', 'Mon Cheri', 'Montezuma', 'Morning Sun', 'Mr. Lincoln', 'Nevada', 'New Beginning', 'New Day', 'New Year', 'Oklahoma', 'Oldtimer', 'Ole', 'Olympiad', 'Oregold', 'Paradise', 'Pascali', 'Peace', 'Perfume Delight', 'Picture', 'Pink Grootendorst', 'Prima Dona', 'Pristine', 'Prominent', 'Promise', 'Proud Land', 'Queen Elizabeth', 'Razzle Dazzle', 'Redgold', 'Rhonda', 'Robin Hood', 'Rocky', 'Royal Highness', 'Sarabande', 'Saratoga', 'Sea Foam', 'Sexy Rexy', 'Sheer Bliss', 'Silk Hat', 'Simplicity', 'Snowfire', 'Sonia', 'Spartan', 'Sterling Silver', 'Summer Sunshine', 'Sun Flare', 'Sunsprite', 'The Fairy', 'Tiffany', 'Touch of Class', 'Tournament of Roses', 'Tropicana', 'Trumpeter', 'Tuxedo', 'Voodoo', 'White Lightnin', 'Will Scarlet', 'Yankee Doodle'

Rosa arkansa
Rosa chinensis 'Manetti'
Rosa davidii
Rosa eglanteria
Rosa foetedia 'Bicolor'
Rosa rugosa 'Rubra'
Rosmarinus officinalis
Rubus deliciosus
Salix babylonica
Salix matsudana 'Tortuosa'
Sambucus caerulea
Sapium sebiferum
Sarcocca ruscifolia
Sequoia sempervirens 'Albo-Spica',
 'Aptos Blue', 'Santa Cruz', 'Soquel',
 seedlings
Sequoiadendron giganteum
Skimmia japonica
Sophora japonica
Spiraea vanhouttei
Stachyurus praecox
Stewartia koreana
Stewartia pseudocamellia
Styrax japonicus
Symphocarpicos albus
Syringa reticulata
Syringa vulgaris 'Charles Joly'
Syzygium paniculatum
Taxodium distichum
Taxus baccata 'Fastigata'
Taxus media 'Kelseyi'
Thuja occidentalis 'Rhinegold', 'Sher-
 wood Moss', 'Stoneham Gold'
Thuja plicata

Thujopsis dolabrata 'nana'
Tibouchina urvilleana
Torreya californica
Trachelospermum jasmoides
Tsuga canadensis 'Mitch Seedling #2',
 'Pendula'
Umbellularia californica
Vaccinium ovatum
Vancouveria hexandra
Vibrunum carlcephalum
Vibrunum davidii
Vibrunum lantana
Vibrunum plicatum tomentosum
 'Shasta', 'Pink Beauty'
Vibrunum tinus 'Spring Boquet'
Vinca major
Walnut (Juglans regia) 'Amigo',
 'Carmello', 'Franquette', 'Hartley'
Weigelia florida 'Variegata'
Wisteria floribunda japonica,
 'Longissima Alba', purple, pink, blue
Wisteria sinensis 'Caroline' blue, pink,
 'Cook's Double Purple', white
Yucca alonifolia

About Tarthang Tulku

Formally educated in the Buddhist tradition in Tibet, Tarthang Tulku is renowned as an innovative teacher and a visionary, independent thinker. He has lived in America for more than twenty years, where he has directed major educational and publishing projects. He is founder and creator of Odiyan Copper Mountain Mandala, a retreat center located in the rolling hills along the coastline of northern California.